Detailed Guide for Your Creativity with Needle Tatting Necklaces

A Guidebook for Beginners

Dempsey W Darryl

THIS BOOK BELONGS TO
The Library of

....

....

Thank you for Purchasing my book and taking the time to read it from front to back. I am always grateful when a reader chooses my work and I hope you enjoyed it!

With the vast selection available online, I am touched that you chose to be purchasing my work and take valuable time out of your life to read it. My hope is that you feel you made the right decision.

I very much would like to know what you thought of the book. Please take the time to write an honest and informative review on Amazon.com. Your experience and opinions will be of great benefit to me and those readers looking to make an informed choice.

With much thanks.

Table of Contents

SUMMARY

What is the Tatting: Tatting is a delicate and intricate form of lace-making that involves creating knots and loops using a small shuttle or a needle. It is a traditional craft that has been practiced for centuries and is still popular today among artisans and hobbyists.

The process of tatting involves working with a continuous thread to create a series of knots and loops that form a pattern. The thread is wound onto a shuttle or threaded through a needle, and the knots are formed by passing the shuttle or needle through loops of thread that have been previously made.

Tatting can be done using various materials, such as cotton, silk, or synthetic threads. The choice of thread can affect the final appearance and texture of the lace. Additionally, beads or other embellishments can be incorporated into the design to add further decorative elements.

One of the defining characteristics of tatting is the use of double stitches, also known as double knots or double stitches. These stitches are created by wrapping the thread around the shuttle or needle multiple times before pulling it through the loop. This technique allows for the creation of intricate patterns and designs.

Tatting can be used to create a wide range of items, including doilies, edgings, jewelry, and even clothing. The lace produced through tatting is known for its delicate and intricate appearance, with patterns often featuring floral motifs, geometric shapes, or intricate lacework.

While tatting can be a time-consuming and meticulous craft, it offers a sense of satisfaction and accomplishment when a beautiful piece of lace is completed. It requires patience and attention to detail, as each knot and loop must be carefully executed to achieve the desired result.

In recent years, tatting has experienced a resurgence in popularity, with many individuals rediscovering the beauty and artistry of this traditional craft. There are numerous resources available, including books, online tutorials, and workshops, that can help beginners learn the basics of tatting and develop their skills.

Overall, tatting is a timeless and elegant craft that allows individuals to create beautiful and intricate lacework. Whether pursued as a hobby or as a professional pursuit, tatting offers a creative outlet and a way to preserve and celebrate the art of lace-making.

Discovering the Art of Tatting: Discovering the Art of Tatting is a fascinating journey into the world of a delicate and intricate form of lace-making. Tatting is a technique that involves creating knots and loops using a small shuttle or needle, resulting in beautiful and intricate designs. This art form has a rich history and has been practiced for centuries, with its origins dating back to the 19th century.

The process of tatting involves working with a thread or yarn and creating a series of knots and loops to form a pattern. The knots are made by passing the shuttle or needle through the loops, creating a secure and decorative stitch. This technique allows for the creation of intricate lace designs, ranging from simple motifs to complex and elaborate patterns.

One of the unique aspects of tatting is that it can be done using either a shuttle or a needle. The shuttle method involves winding the thread around a small shuttle and using it to create the knots and loops. The needle method, on the other hand, involves using a small needle to create the knots and loops directly on the thread. Both methods have their own advantages and can produce stunning results.

Discovering the Art of Tatting not only explores the techniques and tools used in this craft but also delves into the history and cultural significance of tatting. This art form has been practiced by various cultures around the world, each adding their own unique style and patterns to the craft. From Europe to Asia, tatting has been used to create intricate lace trims, doilies, and even jewelry.

The book also provides step-by-step instructions and patterns for beginners to get started with tatting. It covers the basic knots and techniques, as well as more advanced stitches and patterns. The detailed instructions are accompanied by clear illustrations and photographs, making it easy for readers to follow along and create their own beautiful tatting projects.

In addition to the practical aspects of tatting, Discovering the Art of Tatting also explores the artistic and creative possibilities of this craft. It showcases the work of talented tatting artists from around the world, highlighting their unique styles and innovative designs. The book also provides inspiration for readers to experiment with their own ideas and create their own original tatting patterns.

Whether you are a beginner looking to learn a new craft or an experienced tatter looking for inspiration, Discovering the Art of Tatting is a comprehensive guide that will take you on a journey through the history, techniques, and creative possibilities of this beautiful art form.

Essential Tools and Materials of Tatting: Tatting is a delicate and intricate form of lace-making that requires a specific set of tools and materials to create beautiful designs. Whether you are a beginner or an experienced tatter, having the essential tools and materials is crucial for a successful tatting project.

One of the most important tools for tatting is a tatting shuttle. This small, handheld device is used to hold the thread and create the knots and loops that form the lace. Shuttles can be made of various materials such as plastic, metal, or wood, and they come in different shapes and sizes to accommodate different techniques and preferences. Some tatters prefer using a shuttle with a hook, while others prefer a shuttle without a hook. It is important to choose a shuttle that feels comfortable in your hand and suits your tatting style.

In addition to a shuttle, a tatting needle is another tool that can be used for tatting. A tatting needle is a long, thin needle with a small eye at one end. It is used to create the knots and loops by pulling the thread through the stitches. Tatting needles are available in different sizes, and the size you choose depends on the thickness of the thread you are using and the desired outcome of your project. Some tatters prefer using a needle over a shuttle because it allows for more flexibility and control in creating intricate designs.

Apart from the tools, the choice of thread is also crucial in tatting. Traditionally, tatting was done using fine cotton thread, but nowadays, tatters have a wide range of options to choose from. Threads made of cotton, silk, or synthetic materials are commonly used in tatting. The thickness of the thread will determine the size and appearance of the lace. Thicker threads create a bolder and more substantial lace, while thinner threads result in delicate and intricate designs. It is important to choose a thread that is suitable for the desired outcome of your project and that works well with your chosen tool, whether it be a shuttle or a needle.

In addition to the basic tools and materials, there are also various accessories that can enhance the tatting experience. These include a thread winder or bobbin, which helps to keep the thread organized and prevents tangling, and a magnifying glass or lighted magnifier for those who need assistance with close-up work. Some tatters also use a foam pad or a tatting pillow to provide a soft surface for their work and to prevent the shuttle or needle from slipping.

Setting Up Your Tatting Workspace of Tatting: Setting up your tatting workspace is an essential step in ensuring a comfortable and efficient tatting experience. Whether you are a beginner or an experienced tatter, having a well-organized and well-equipped workspace can greatly enhance your creativity and productivity.

First and foremost, you need to find a suitable location for your tatting workspace. Ideally, it should be a quiet and well-lit area where you can concentrate on your work without any distractions. A corner of your living room, a spare room, or even a dedicated craft room can serve as a perfect spot for your tatting endeavors.

Once you have chosen the location, it's time to think about the furniture and storage options for your workspace. A sturdy table or desk is a must-have, as it will provide you with a stable surface to work on. Make sure it is at a comfortable height for you to sit or stand, depending on your preference. Additionally, consider investing in a comfortable chair that provides adequate support for your back to prevent any discomfort during long tatting sessions.

Next, you need to organize your tatting supplies and tools. A dedicated storage system, such as a set of drawers or plastic containers, can help you keep your threads, shuttles, and other accessories neatly organized and easily accessible. Sort your threads by color or type, and label each container accordingly to save time when searching for specific materials.

In addition to storage, it's important to have a good lighting setup in your workspace. Natural light is ideal, so try to position your workspace near a window. However, if natural light is not sufficient, invest in a good quality desk lamp with adjustable brightness and direction to ensure optimal visibility of your work.

Another crucial aspect of setting up your tatting workspace is having a comfortable and ergonomic setup. Consider using a wrist rest or cushion to support your hands and wrists while tatting, as this can help prevent strain and fatigue. Additionally, make sure your workspace is clutter-free, with enough space to move your hands and tools freely.

Lastly, don't forget to personalize your workspace to make it inspiring and enjoyable. Hang up some artwork or photographs that inspire you, or display your finished tatting projects as a reminder of your progress and achievements. Surrounding yourself with things that bring you joy and motivation can greatly enhance your tatting experience.

In conclusion, setting up your tatting workspace involves careful consideration of the location, furniture, storage, lighting, ergonomics, and personalization.

Understanding Tatting Patterns and Diagrams: Understanding Tatting Patterns and Diagrams is essential for anyone interested in the art of tatting. Tatting is a technique used to create delicate and intricate lace designs using a small shuttle or needle. It involves making a series of knots and loops with thread to form decorative patterns.

Tatting patterns and diagrams are the visual representations of the designs that tatters follow to create their lacework. These patterns can range from simple and beginner-friendly to complex and advanced. They provide a step-by-step guide on how to create each knot and loop, allowing tatters to replicate the design accurately.

To understand tatting patterns and diagrams, it is important to familiarize oneself with the various symbols and notations used in the craft. Each symbol represents a specific action or stitch, such as a double stitch, picot, or chain. By understanding these symbols, tatters can decipher the instructions provided in the pattern and execute the desired design.

One of the key elements in understanding tatting patterns and diagrams is recognizing the repeat sequences. Many patterns have repeat sections, where a specific set of stitches is repeated multiple times to create the overall design. By identifying these repeat sequences, tatters can save time and effort by memorizing the pattern and executing it more efficiently.

Another aspect to consider when understanding tatting patterns and diagrams is the importance of tension and gauge. Tension refers to the tightness or looseness of the stitches, while gauge refers to the size of the finished piece. Both factors can significantly impact the final outcome of the design. It is crucial for tatters to maintain consistent tension throughout their work to ensure uniformity in their stitches and achieve the desired gauge.

Additionally, understanding the terminology used in tatting patterns and diagrams is essential. Terms such as "ring," "chain," "join," and "picot" are commonly used and refer to specific actions or stitches in the tatting process. Familiarizing oneself with these terms will help tatters follow the instructions accurately and avoid confusion.

Lastly, practice and patience are key when it comes to understanding tatting patterns and diagrams. Like any skill, it takes time and effort to become proficient in reading and executing these patterns. Tatters should start with simpler designs and gradually progress to more complex ones as they gain confidence and experience.

In conclusion, understanding tatting patterns and diagrams is crucial for anyone interested in the art of tatting. By familiarizing oneself with the symbols, repeat sequences, tension, gauge, terminology, and practicing regularly,…

Traditional Tatting Styles: Traditional tatting styles refer to the various techniques and patterns that have been passed down through generations in the art of tatting. Tatting is a form of lace-making that involves creating intricate designs using a series of knots and loops. It is a delicate and time-consuming craft that requires precision and attention to detail.

One of the most well-known traditional tatting styles is the shuttle tatting technique. This technique involves using a small shuttle, usually made of metal or plastic, to create the knots and loops that form the lace. The shuttle is threaded with a length of thread or yarn, and the knots are created by wrapping the thread around the shuttle and pulling it through loops that have been formed on a base thread. This technique allows for greater control and precision in creating the intricate patterns that are characteristic of traditional tatting.

Another traditional tatting style is needle tatting. This technique involves using a small, pointed needle to create the knots and loops. The needle is threaded with a length of thread or yarn, and the knots are created by passing the needle through loops that have been formed on a base thread. Needle tatting allows for more flexibility and creativity in creating designs, as the needle can be easily manipulated to create different shapes and patterns.

Traditional tatting styles also include various patterns and motifs that are commonly used in tatting. These patterns can range from simple geometric shapes to more intricate floral and lace designs. Some popular motifs include flowers, leaves, hearts, and butterflies. These motifs can be combined and arranged in different ways to create unique and beautiful designs.

In addition to the techniques and patterns, traditional tatting styles also involve the use of different materials and tools. The thread or yarn used in tatting can vary in thickness and texture, depending on the desired effect. Common materials include cotton, silk, and synthetic fibers. The tools used in tatting include shuttles, needles, and various types of hooks and pins.

Traditional tatting styles have a rich history and cultural significance. They have been practiced by different cultures around the world for centuries, and each culture has its own unique style and techniques. In some cultures, tatting is considered a form of art and is used to create intricate and decorative pieces for clothing, accessories, and home decor. In other cultures, tatting is a traditional craft that is passed down through generations as a way to preserve cultural heritage and traditions.

Modern and Contemporary Tatting: Modern and contemporary tatting is a form of lace-making that has evolved and adapted to the changing times. It combines traditional techniques with innovative designs and materials to create unique and stunning pieces of art.

One of the defining characteristics of modern and contemporary tatting is the use of unconventional materials. While traditional tatting was typically done with thread or yarn, modern tatting artists have expanded their repertoire to include materials such as wire, beads, and even paper. This allows for greater creativity and experimentation, as artists can incorporate different textures and colors into their work.

In addition to materials, modern tatting also incorporates new techniques and patterns. While traditional tatting patterns often featured intricate motifs and delicate lacework, contemporary tatting artists have pushed the boundaries of the craft by creating more abstract and geometric designs. They also use techniques such as split rings and split chains, which allow for more complex and intricate patterns to be created.

Another aspect of modern and contemporary tatting is the incorporation of technology. With the advent of computer-aided design (CAD) software and 3D printing, tatting artists can now create intricate patterns and designs that were once impossible to achieve by hand. This opens up a whole new world of possibilities for tatting artists, as they can now create three-dimensional pieces and experiment with different shapes and structures.

Furthermore, modern tatting has also embraced the concept of sustainability and eco-friendliness. Many contemporary tatting artists use recycled materials or organic fibers in their work, reducing their environmental impact and promoting a more sustainable approach to art-making. This not only adds an additional layer of meaning to their creations but also aligns with the growing global movement towards sustainability.

Overall, modern and contemporary tatting is a vibrant and dynamic art form that continues to evolve and push the boundaries of traditional lace-making. It combines traditional techniques with innovative materials, patterns, and technology to create unique and visually stunning pieces of art. Whether it's through the use of unconventional materials, intricate patterns, or sustainable practices, modern tatting artists are constantly finding new ways to express their creativity and leave their mark on the world of lace-making.

Common Tatting Mistakes and How to Fix Them:

A Comprehensive Guide

Introduction:

Tatting is a delicate and intricate craft that involves creating beautiful lace-like designs using a shuttle or a needle. While it may seem intimidating at first, with practice and patience, anyone can master the art of tatting. However, like any other craft, mistakes are bound to happen along the way. In this guide, we will explore some of the most common tatting mistakes and provide you with detailed solutions on how to fix them, ensuring that your tatting projects turn out flawless every time.

1. Uneven Tension:

One of the most prevalent mistakes in tatting is uneven tension, which can result in an unbalanced and messy finished product. Uneven tension occurs when the thread is pulled too tightly or too loosely, causing inconsistencies in the size and shape of the knots. To fix this, it is crucial to practice maintaining a consistent tension throughout your work. Take breaks if needed, and always check your tension by gently tugging on the thread after each knot. If you notice any inconsistencies, adjust your tension accordingly.

2. Miscounting Stitches:

Another common mistake in tatting is miscounting stitches, leading to an irregular pattern or design. This can be frustrating, especially when working on intricate projects. To avoid miscounting stitches, it is essential to carefully follow the pattern instructions and use stitch markers or highlighters to keep track of your progress. If you do make a mistake, don't panic. Simply undo the incorrect stitches and retrace your steps back to the point of error. Taking your time and double-checking your work will help minimize the chances of miscounting stitches.

3. Knots Getting Tangled:

Tangled knots are a common frustration in tatting, often occurring when the thread becomes twisted or knotted during the process. To prevent this, make sure to keep your thread untangled and smooth as you work. If you notice any knots forming, stop immediately and gently untangle them using a needle or your fingers. Additionally, using a thread conditioner or lightly waxing your thread can help reduce friction and prevent tangling. Taking these precautions will save you time and frustration in the long run.

4. Inconsistent Picots:

Picots are small loops that add decorative elements to tatting designs. However, achieving consistent picots can be challenging, especially for beginners. Inconsistent picots can make your work appear messy and unprofessional.

Tips for Tatting Success:

Tatting is a beautiful and intricate form of lace-making that requires patience, precision, and practice. Whether you are a beginner or have some experience with tatting, here are some tips to help you achieve success in this delicate craft.

1. Start with the right tools: To begin your tatting journey, you will need a tatting shuttle or a tatting needle. Choose a shuttle or needle that feels comfortable in your hand and suits your personal preference. Additionally, make sure to have a good pair of scissors, a crochet hook, and some thread or yarn suitable for tatting.

2. Learn the basic techniques: Familiarize yourself with the basic tatting techniques before attempting more complex patterns. Start by learning how to make a double stitch, also known as a double knot or a double stitch ring. Practice this stitch until you can create consistent and even knots.

3. Choose the right thread: The type of thread you use can greatly impact the outcome of your tatting project. Opt for a thread that is smooth, strong, and easy to work with. Size 20 or 30 cotton thread is commonly used for tatting, but you can experiment with different thread sizes and materials to achieve different effects.

4. Practice tension control: Maintaining consistent tension is crucial in tatting. Too loose tension can result in sloppy and uneven stitches, while too tight tension can make it difficult to work with the thread. Practice finding the right balance and adjust your tension as needed to create neat and uniform stitches.

5. Start with simple patterns: As a beginner, it is best to start with simple patterns that involve fewer elements and techniques. This will help you build your skills and confidence before moving on to more complex designs. Look for beginner-friendly patterns that include clear instructions and diagrams to guide you through the process.

6. Take breaks and be patient: Tatting requires a lot of concentration and fine motor skills. It is important to take breaks and rest your hands and eyes to avoid fatigue. Remember that tatting is a slow and meticulous craft, so be patient with yourself and enjoy the process of creating something beautiful stitch by stitch.

7. Join a tatting community: Connecting with other tatting enthusiasts can be a great source of inspiration, support, and learning. Join online forums, social media groups, or local tatting clubs to share your work, ask questions, and learn from experienced tatters.

Finishing and Displaying Your Tatting Projects: Finishing and displaying your tatting projects is an important step in the creative process. It not only adds the final touches to your work but also allows you to showcase your talent and share your creations with others. In this guide, we will explore various techniques and ideas to help you effectively finish and display your tatting projects.

Firstly, let's discuss the finishing process. Once you have completed your tatting project, it is essential to secure the loose ends and ensure that all the knots and stitches are secure. This can be done by carefully weaving in the loose ends using a small crochet hook or a tapestry needle. Take your time and be gentle to avoid damaging the delicate tatting work. Once all the loose ends are secured, you can trim any excess thread, leaving a neat and clean finish.

Next, let's move on to displaying your tatting projects. There are numerous ways to showcase your work, depending on the size and nature of the project. One popular option is to frame your tatting piece. This can be done by placing the tatting on a piece of acid-free mat board and securing it with archival tape or glue. Then, choose a frame that complements your tatting and carefully mount it. This method not only protects your work but also allows you to hang it on a wall or display it on a shelf.

Another creative way to display your tatting projects is by incorporating them into functional items. For example, you can attach your tatting to a plain pillowcase, tablecloth, or even a clothing item like a scarf or a handkerchief. This adds a unique and personalized touch to everyday items and allows you to showcase your tatting skills in a practical way.

If you prefer a more portable option, consider creating a display case or a shadow box. These can be made using a wooden or acrylic box with a glass front. Arrange your tatting inside the box, ensuring that it is securely attached. You can add additional elements like fabric or lace to enhance the overall presentation. Display cases and shadow boxes are great for exhibiting multiple tatting projects or creating themed displays.

For smaller tatting projects, such as earrings or pendants, consider using jewelry displays. These can be found in various shapes and sizes, including stands, trays, or even wall-mounted organizers. Choose a display that suits your style and preferences, and arrange your tatting pieces in an appealing manner.

INTRODUCTION

Finally, after many tries and unsuccessful attempts, after many hours looking for a solution to make the necklace, I managed to decipher how to create it.

This is an opportunity to be immersed in artisans or training centers for crafts. Needle tatting technique is more recent. But be careful to choose special tatting needles to be sure you have the right equipment for this technique. For example, a mattress needle is not suitable

for tatting: its eye is too big to form knots and its tip is too sharp to handle it easily.

CHAPTER ONE

THE DIY OF TATTING NECKLACE (1 / 15 STEPS)

Step 1: Needle beads & adding beads

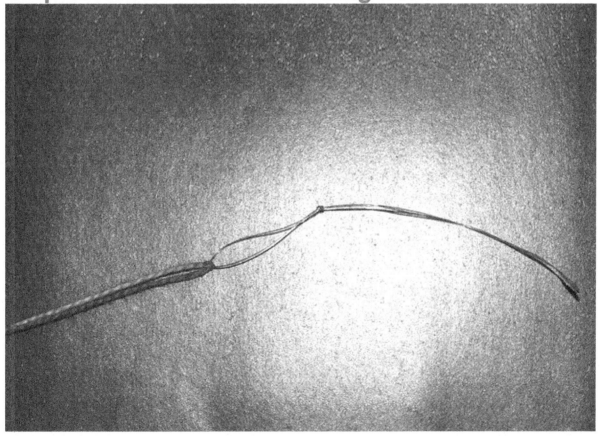

This first step is very important!

Before starting the work, we must introduce all the beads in the thread that are going to be needed for our work. The beads remain in the ball thread, waiting to be used when needed.

Remark:

If we are unsure of the exact total amount of beads we need to work on, you should be sure and make several more beads. It is better for us on pearls that we are not missing.

To enter the beads into the thread, I use several hours in search of a needle that will suffice appropriate, but none of the people I have had in my house have gone well. So I decided to create my own beading needle.

It's very simple: We take a piece of thin nylon peach thread, between 7 and 10 cm long, fold it in half and make a knot with the two ropes by half the length. Then gently and with the help of a lighter, heat the ends of the two to melt the nylon strings and press between your fingers to unite them. Ideally we would be like you see in the picture.

Step 2: prepare working materials

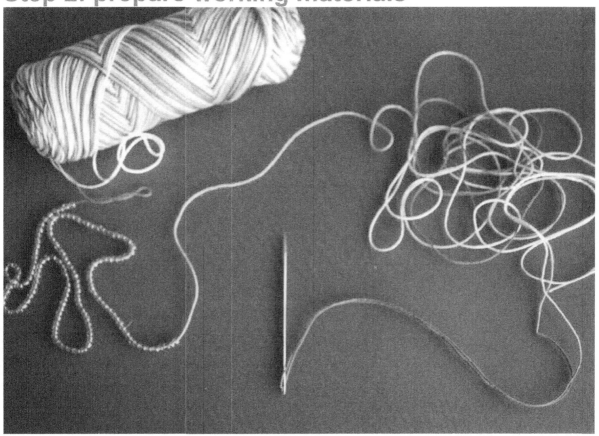

Once you have entered all the beads necessary to work in the thread, pass the thread through the hole of the tatting needle, and we will obtain a color desk that contrasts with the work, to give us a good job.

We have the yarn in the balloon, along with the beads, we are going to use for our work. In the needle we have the thread that we need to pass through inside the stitches of all the works. The thread is the same, but we will start in the middle of the thread, leaving on the right, the needle, all the long thread necessary to assemble the structure of the part. For this reason, we must leave quite a long thread in the needle.

Materials needed:

1 ball of cotton yarn (45 gr)

1 needle beads (I explain how to do it in the previous step)

1 tatting needle (size according to your yarn size)

1 crochet hook (size according to your wire size)

100 crystal beads approximately (not recommended plastic beads, because if you need iron for work they can be wrong)

Remark:

Try to choose a range of colors for yarn and counts, to coordinate properly.

THE DIY OF TATTING NECKLACE (3 / 15 STEPS)

Step 3: achieve the double point: first semester

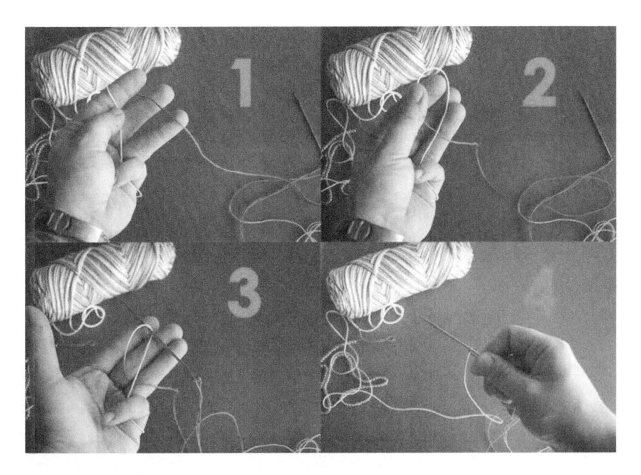

The Double Point

Is the basic point for tatting. It consists of two halves, which are two knots around the needle, the right and the backhand suite, as you can see in this and the next step of the Instruction.

First half of the point

Yarn in left hand is ball. Insert needle as shown, then remove finger and pull yarn tight to put stitch on needle.

CHAPTER TWO

THE DIY OF TATTING NECKLACE (4 / 15 STEPS)

Step 4: make the double stitch: second half

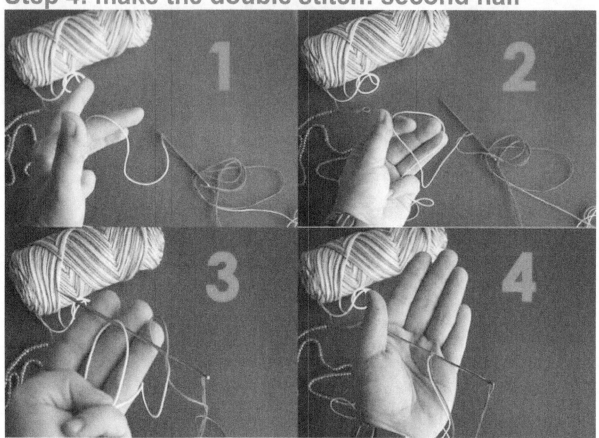

Second half of the point

Insert needle as shown, then remove finger and pull yarn tight to put stitch on needle.

Remark:

It is very important to tighten the stitches, so that the work will be neat and compact, then the stitches, we were not open or stretched more than they should.

Likewise, it is also important to choose the appropriate size of the needle for each thickness of the yarn that we will be using. The needle should never be thicker than the thread of our work.

THE DIY OF TATTING NECKLACE (5 / 15 STEPS)

Step 5: make a picot

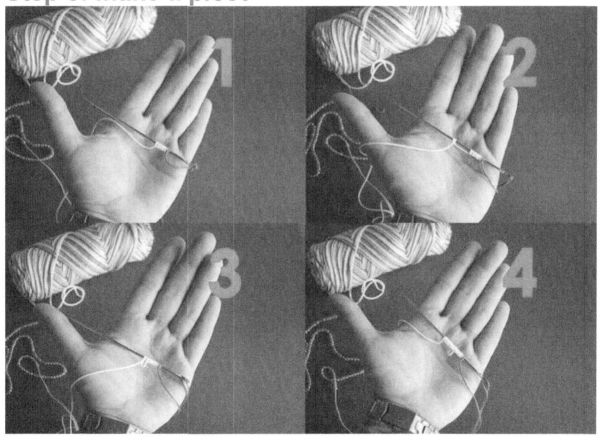

Picot prick (abbrevation. p)

Finish the first half of the stitch as before, but use your right hand finger to keep a space between the stitches already on the needle and the first half of the stitch.

Remark:

The pins are used to join the different shapes and works and are also decorative elements of the piece.

For this reason, when Picot joins pieces, we make it shorter, but since then, going through the Picot yarn and stretching, we also could enlarge the hole and leave the dirty work and poor finish. On the other hand, when Picot serves as decoration, we will do it as long as we want them or dictate the design pattern we do.

THE DIY OF TATTING NECKLACE (6 / 15 STEPS)

Step 6: basic shapes: chains and rings

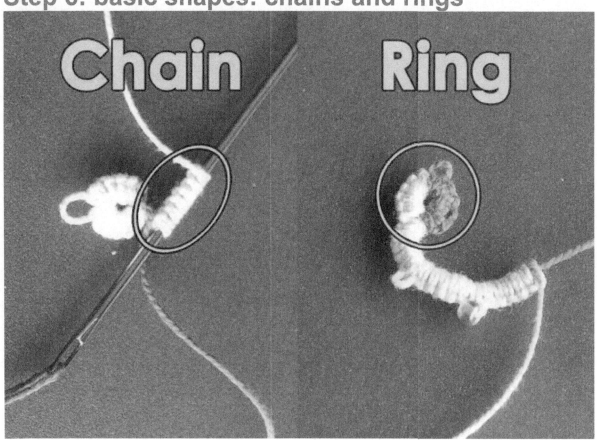

In the art of lace are 2 basic points, the Double point (ds) and the Picot point (p).

These are also the two basic methods for mounting these stitches, the chain (Ch) and the ring (R).

The chain is a series of stitches, through which the thread passes and is not closed.

The ring is a series of stitches, through which the thread passes, closing at the end to form the ring.

Chains and rings can be formed from different stitches in succession, alternating between Double stitch and Picot stitch.

If we can find patterns like these:

Ch-4p2p2p2p4-yo (yo is spun, thanks to the inside of the dots)

R-6 p 6-Cl (Cl is near the ring)

CHAPTER THREE

THE DIY OF TATTING NECKLACE (7 / 15 STEPS)

Step 7: make a ring

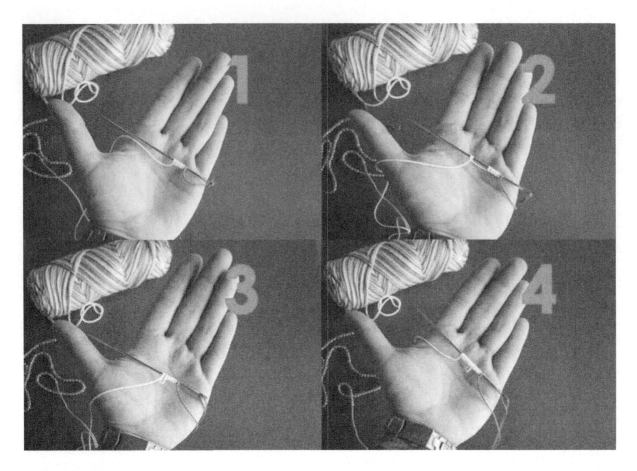

Ring (abbrevation R)

We are going to make our first ring!

First mount ds 6, we have 1 Picot and once again mount ds 6.

Then just close the ring, passing the thread of the needle through the stitches, but with his left hand holding the end of the thread where the work begins, forming a loop through which the needle passes to close the 'ring.

In a model we find well annotated: R-6 p 6-Cl

Remark:

If you look at the images displayed can see how to close the ring in detail.

Step 8: start the necklace!

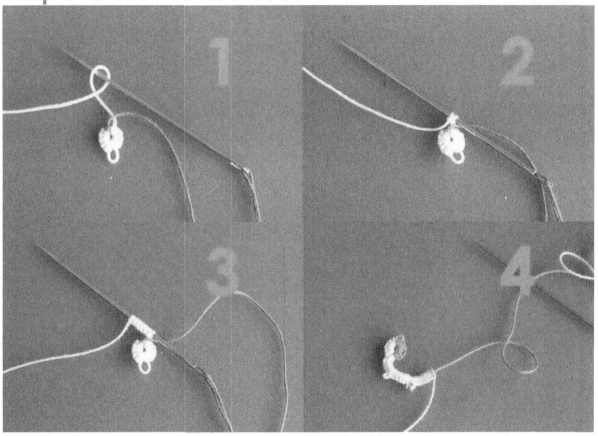

We will start the necklace following the pattern. Continue the pattern instructions:

1 - R-6 p 6-Cl-rw (rw means turn)

2 - ch-6p6B6-yo-rw (B means a bead, which will introduce to work in the same space as a Picot could do)

Notes:

To add a bead, you will only have to pick up the thread of the needle, and then we carry out the following stitches.

At each step of the instruction, adding shorthand notation that you have come home to the most familiar will go.

Also you have the support of photos and illustrations to explain how it should be the shape of the piece you are doing at every moment.

THE DIY OF TATTING NECKLACE (9 / 15 STEPS)

Step 9: second ring & second chain

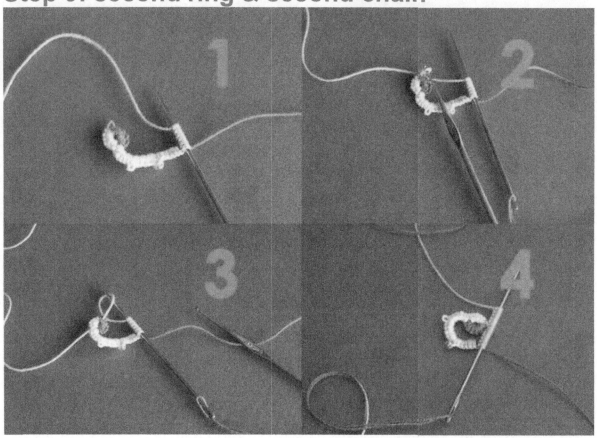

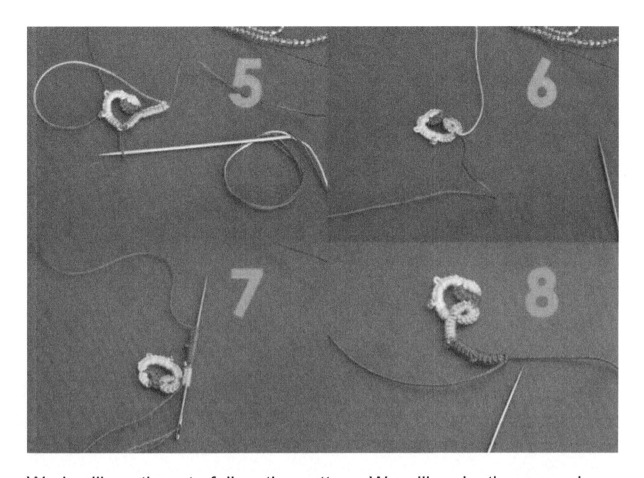

Work will continue to follow the pattern. We will make the second crown, first we put 6 ds on the needle and then replace the Picot, which connects the work on the Picot point of the first ring, therefore, with the help of a crochet needle, pass the yarn from the ball through the Picot stitch of the first ring and put the loop on the needle closer to yarn, then continue to add more 6 ds to the needle and finally close the second ring as usual.

We will continue to make the second chain (remember: we have to examine the work each time), this time add 6 ds first to the needle, then add a bead, plus 6 ds a Picot and 6 ds more and finally, pass the yarn through the needle stitches, to continue the work.

Continue the pattern instructions:

3 - R-6 + 6-Cl-rw

4 - ch-6B6p6-yo-rw

CHAPTER FOUR

THE DIY OF TATTING NECKLACE (10 / 15 STEPS)

Step 10: next steps: the lower part of the necklace

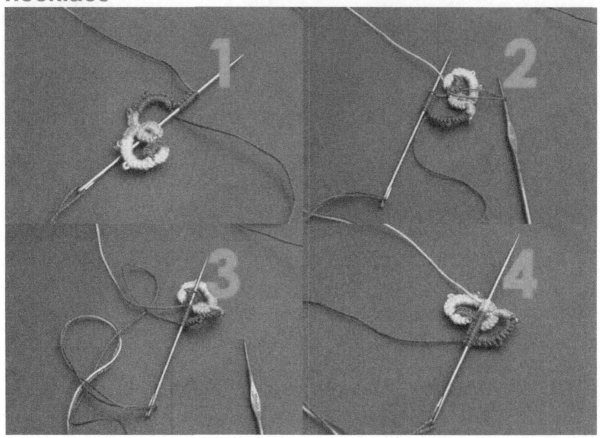

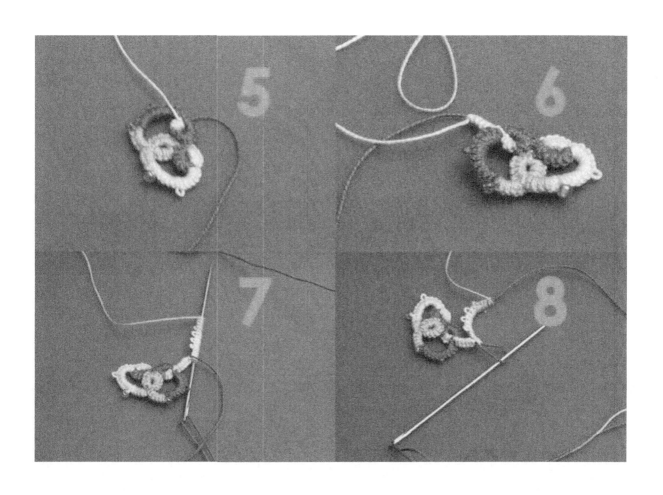

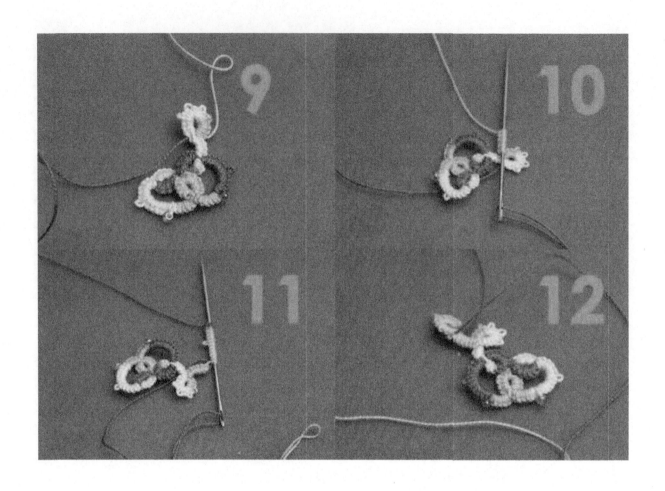

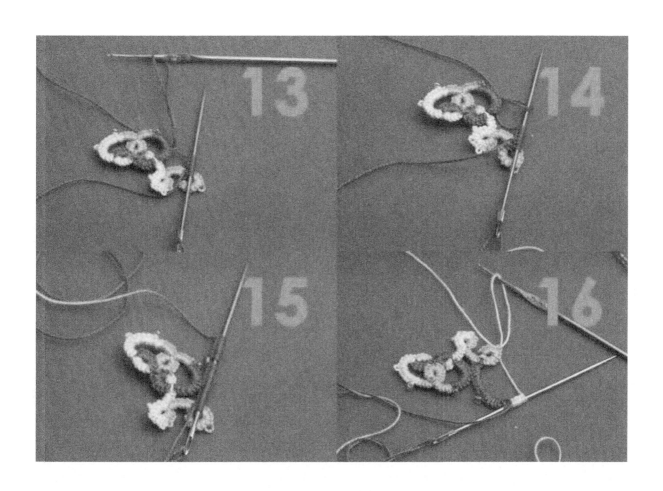

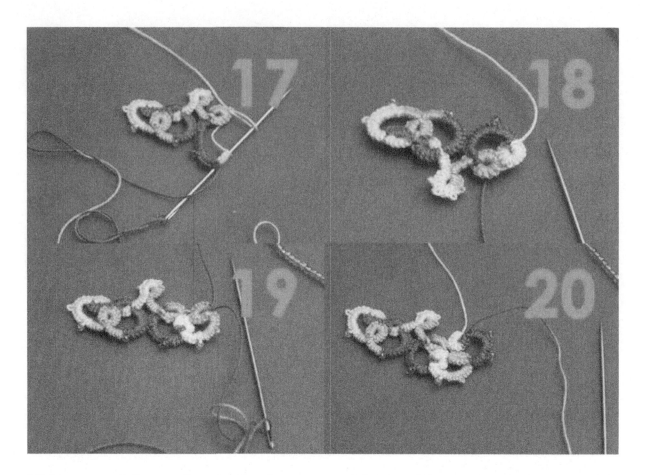

This part of the collar, is the bottom, which willdo go back to finish the job.

The necklace is finished in the middle, but we could change the pattern to finish at one end. For now we will start in this order and the assembly of the first part, which is very useful to go and check the performance the work done correctly all the necessary points and forms.

Continue the pattern instructions:

5 - R-6 + 6-Cl-rw

6 - ch-6-yo-rw

7 - R-4p2p2p2p4-Cl-rw

8 - ch-6-yo-rw

9 - R-6 p 6-Cl-rw

10 - ch-6 + 6 b 6-yo-rw (join the chain with the chain Picot stitch after)

11 - R-6 + 6-Cl-rw (join the ring with the first ring, which n not attached with the others of this part)

12 - ch-6B6p6-yo-rw

13 - R-6 + 6-Cl-rw

THE DIY OF TATTING NECKLACE (11 / 15 STEPS)

Step 11: next steps: the top of the necklace

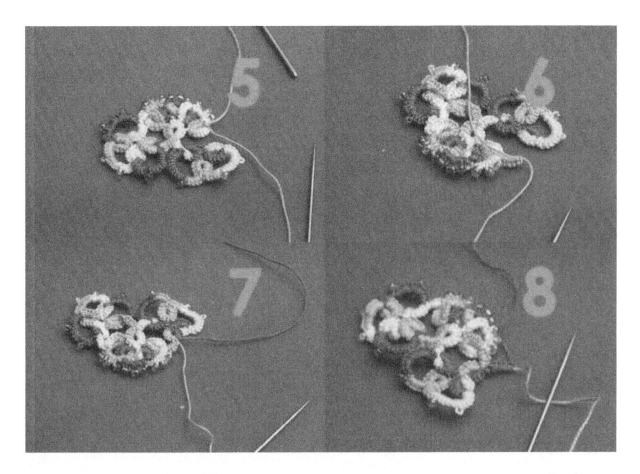

This part of the necklace is up to the top, which will start working, and which will determine the length of our necklace.

Remark :

We must bear in mind that, when tied down, represents a third of their original long. It is for this reason that we should measure the length of the first finished module, to calculate how many modules you need to fill our necklace to the desired length.

Continue the pattern instructions:

14 - ch-6-yo-rw

15 - R-6 + 6-Cl-rw (join yarn with first Picot stitch of large ring with 4 Picots)

16 - ch-2B2B2B2-yo-rw (Repeat 15 to 16 4 times, for any Picot stitch large ring) 17 - ch-6-yo-rw 18 - R-6 + 6-Cl-rw (join the thread with the 3 rings at the bottom part) 19 - ch-6-yo-rw

THE DIY OF TATTING NECKLACE (12 / 15 STEPS)

Step 12: make the top modules

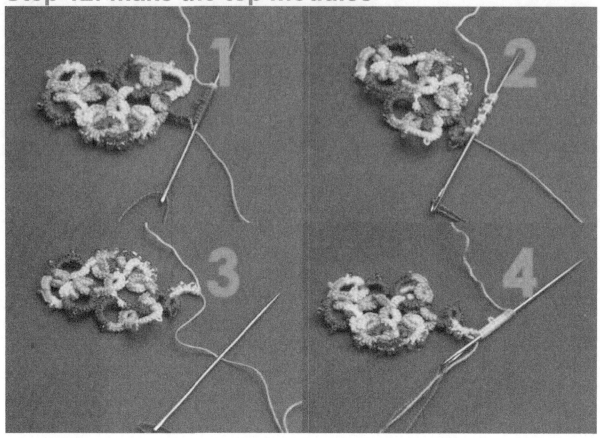

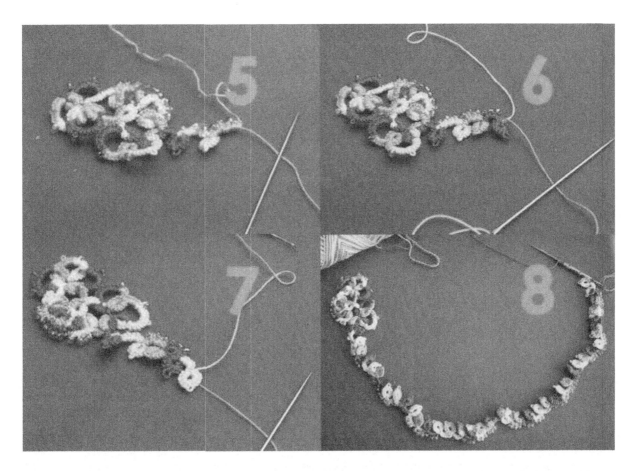

And at this time, when we have finished the first module of the collar, and we will start making the top of the collar, then close the work with the bottom.

From a chain with 6 ds.

Continue the pattern instructions:

19 - ch-6-yo-rw

20 - r-6 p 6-cl-rw

21 - ch-2b2b2b2-yo-rw (20 votes against 21, repeats it 4 times) 22 - ch-6-yo-rw 23 -r - 6p6-cl-rw

Repeat steps 19-23, which form the beginning of a module, as many times as necessary to reach the desired length for our necklace.

CHAPTER FIVE

THE DIY OF TATTING NECKLACE (13 / 15 STEPS)

Step 13: next steps: the lower part of the necklace

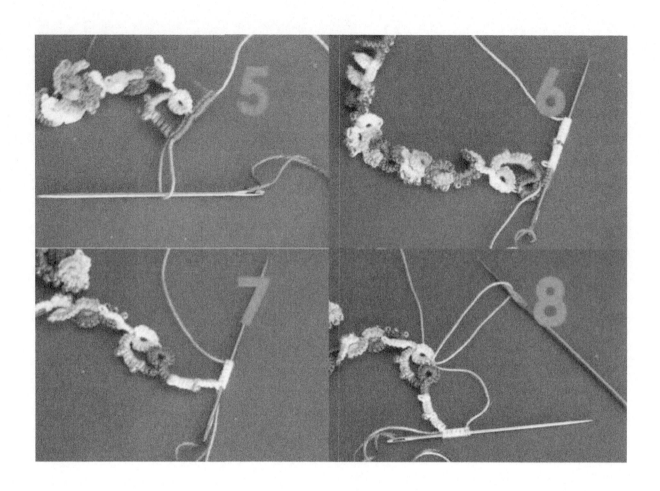

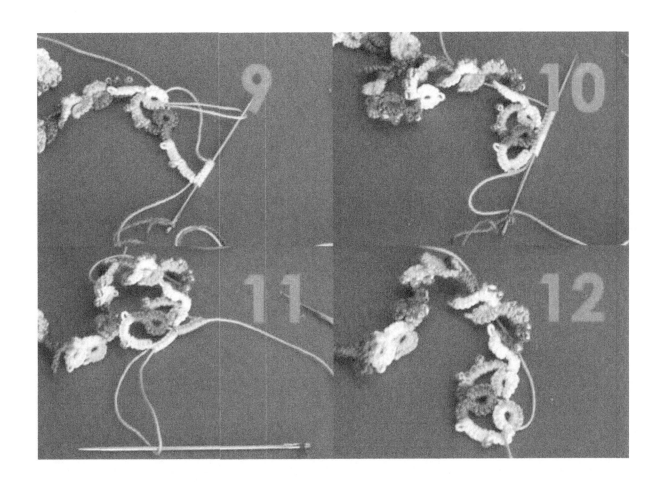

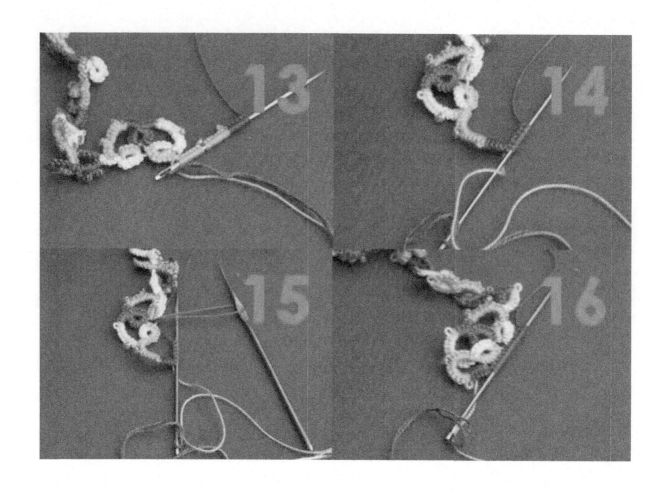

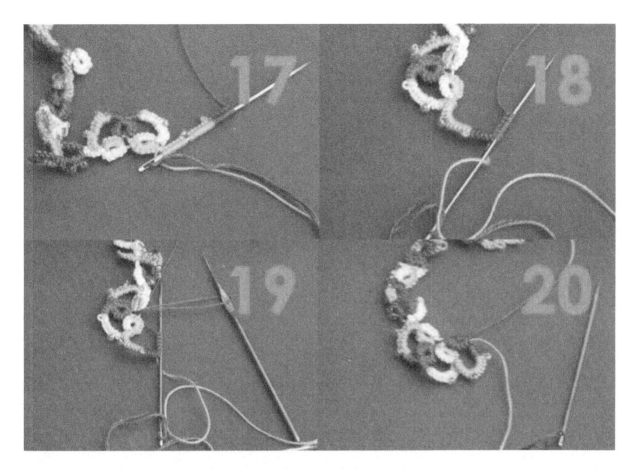

Once we have made the top of our necklace, let's start at the bottom, so that we can close the modules that look good and finish the necklace.

The upper part of the modules is made in step 23, regardless of the number of repeated modules as we need.

First of all, we will close this final module following the same model set up in the initial module.

We will continue with the model:

24 - ch-6B6p6-yp-rw

25 - R-6 + 6-Cl-rw

26 - ch-6p6B6-yo-rw

27 - R-6 + 6-Cl-rw

28 - ch-6B6p6-yo-rw

29 - R-6 + 6-Cl-rw

THE DIY OF TATTING NECKLACE (14 / 15 STEPS)

Step 14: make the bottom part of the modules

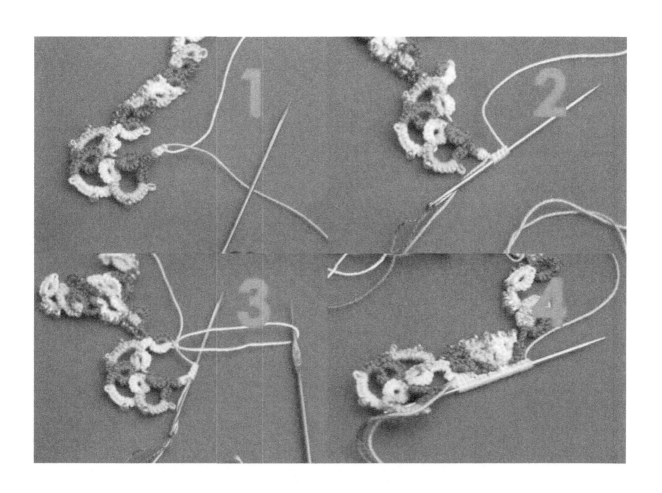

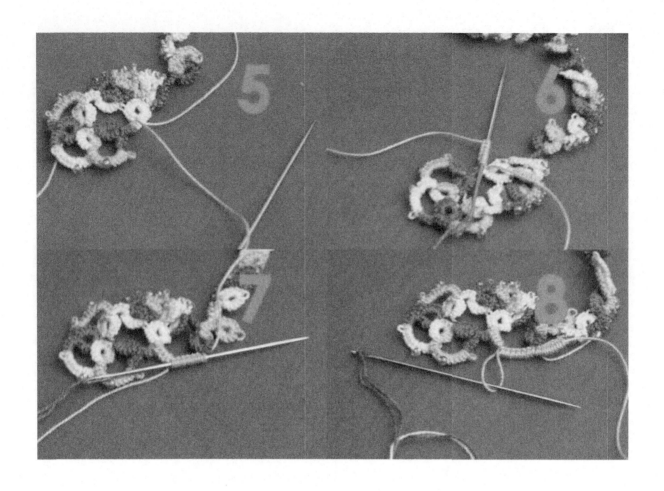

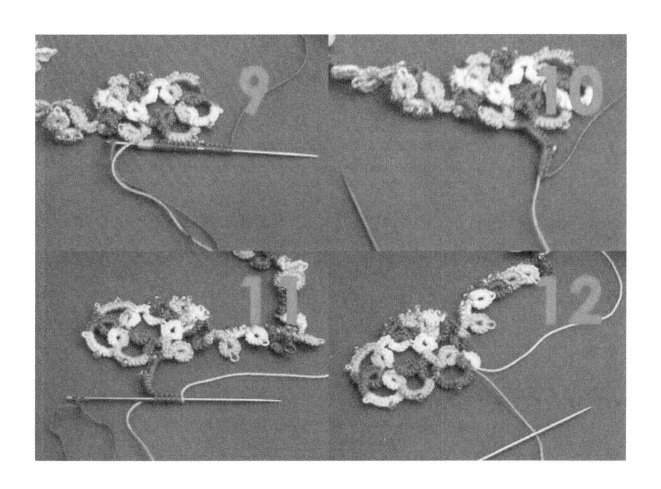

And finally, we have come to the beginning of the end of our work. The bottom of the modules.

This is by uniting the various rings on top, following the pattern established in the modules at both ends of the necklace.

We will continue the pattern:

30 - ch-6-yo-rw

31 - R-4 + 2 + 2 + 2 + 4-Cl-rw (here we make the large ring, connecting the 4 ring pins at the top of the module, closing at the end as d habit in the rings)

32 - ch-6-yo-rw

33 - R-6 + 6-Cl-rw (this ring must join the central ring is located between the modules)

34 - ch-6 + 6 b 6-yo-rw (this chain is linked to the Picot point in the chain of the previous module, to join the different modules of the collar)

35 - R-6 + 6-Cl-rw

36 - ch-6B6p6-yo-rw (point Picot of this chain is then join the lower part of the next module)

THE DIY OF TATTING NECKLACE (15 / 15 STEPS)

Step 15: end of necklace

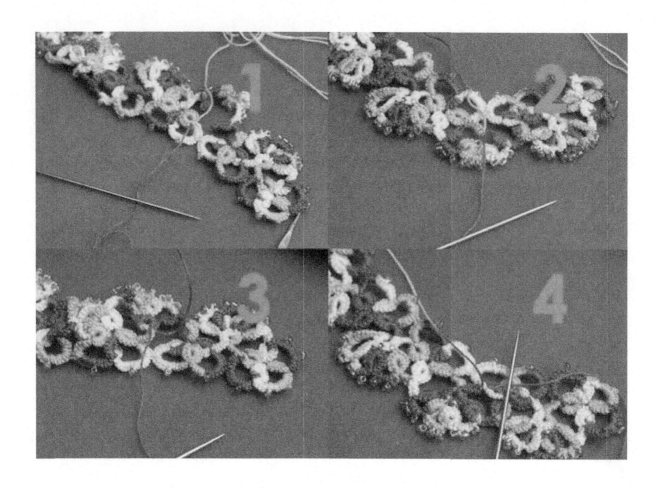

Repeat steps 30-36, which form the bottom of the module, as many times as necessary to end our necklace.

Finally, when you reach the top of the last module still to be reached, finish the job by joining the first module, which we created at the beginning of the pass.

At this time, in step 36, instead of making a Picot stitch, will join the yarn with the Picot stitch from the bottom of the initial collar of the module, so close to the bottom and therefore able to complete the module with the large ring inside.

We will continue the pattern:

36 (special end) -Ch-6 b 6 + 6-yo-rw

37 - R-6 + 6-Cl-rw

38 - ch-6-yo-rw

39 - R-4 + 2 + 2 + 2 + 4 -Cl-rw

40 - ch-6 + (join with initial ring) -yo

MAKE a SMAL knot and cut the thread!

Now we're just going to add the Collar Closures, Pimples Sewing Items left blank at both ends of the collar.

And good luck!

THE END